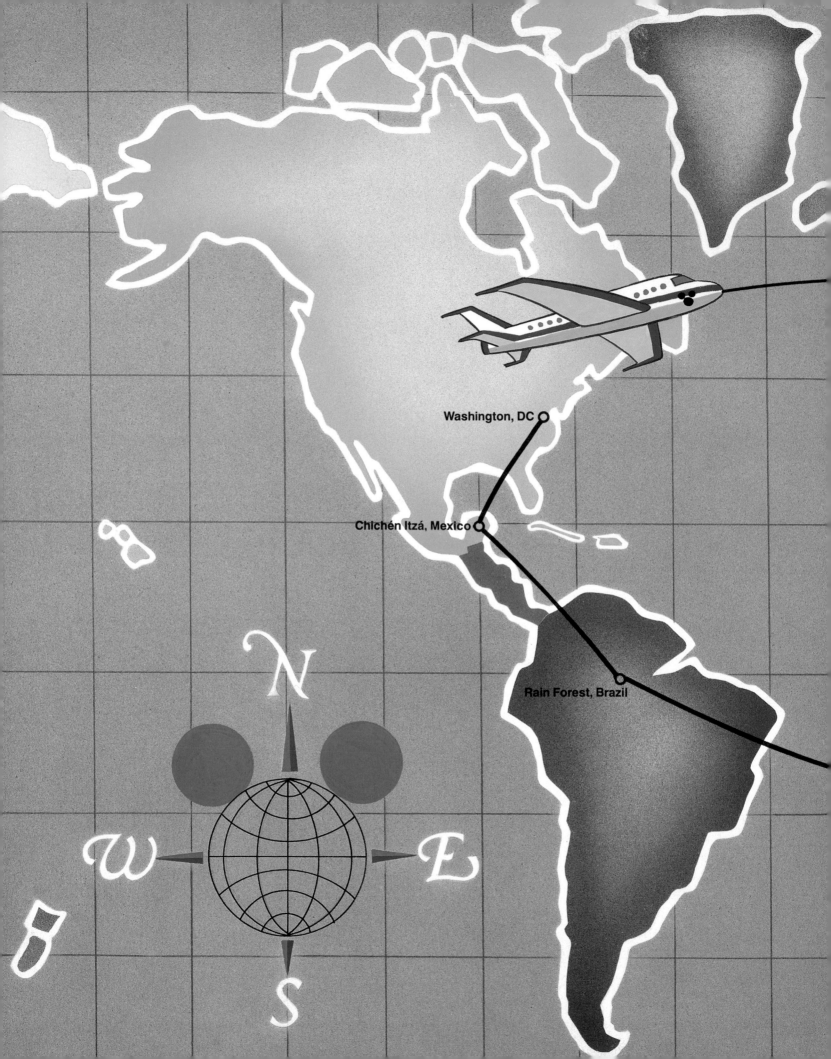

Washington, DC

Chichén Itzá, Mexico

Rain Forest, Brazil

N
W
E
S

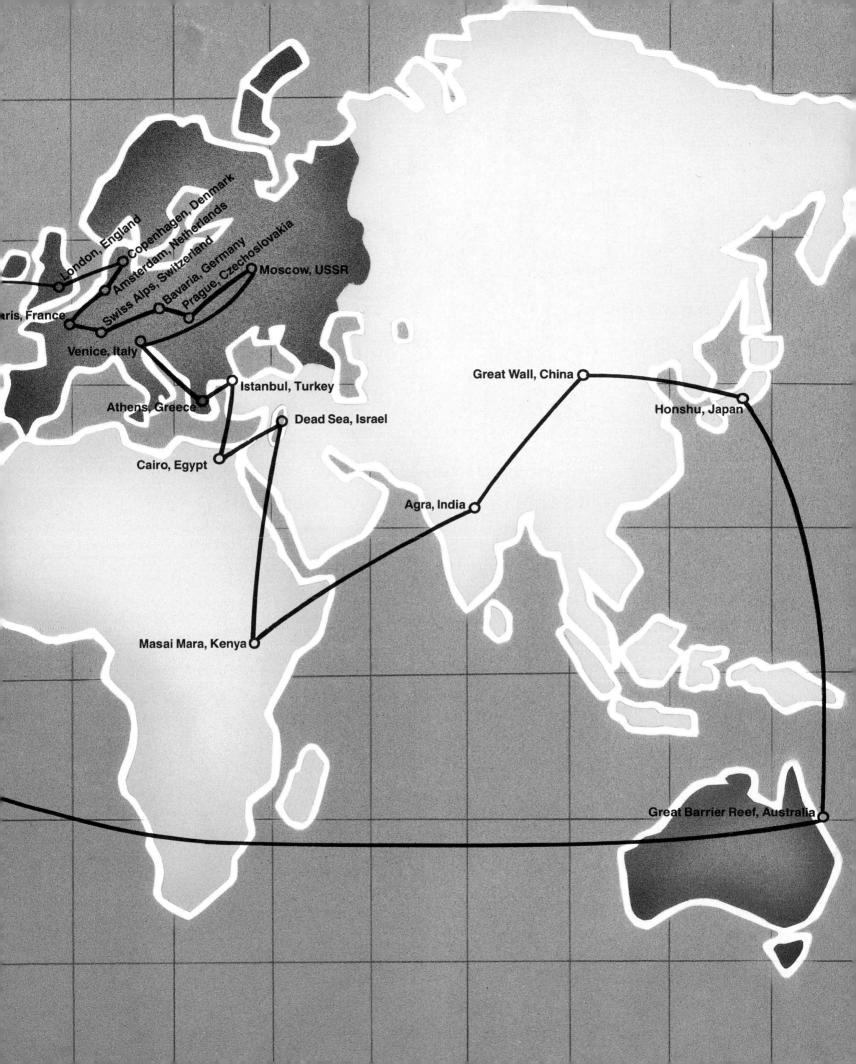

London, England
Copenhagen, Denmark
Amsterdam, Netherlands
Swiss Alps, Switzerland
Bavaria, Germany
Prague, Czechoslovakia
Moscow, USSR
Paris, France
Venice, Italy
Istanbul, Turkey
Athens, Greece
Dead Sea, Israel
Cairo, Egypt
Great Wall, China
Honshu, Japan
Agra, India
Masai Mara, Kenya
Great Barrier Reef, Australia

# Dobry'den!

Dobry'den

(doh-BREE den)

Everyone loves walking across the Charles Bridge in Prague, Czechoslovakia. The bridge has 30 statues on it—and a few hundred swans floating under it!

# Dobryi den!

Do you recognize Red Square in Moscow in the USSR? Just look at all the buildings with the colorful onion-shaped domes!

## Добрый день

Dobryi den

(DOH-bree dehn)

# Buon giorno!

Venice, Italy, is a city of canals. A fun way to get around is by gondola—and you are sure to have a smooth ride unless you let Goofy do the rowing!

Buon giorno

(bwohn JOR-noh)

# Yia-sou!

We're in Athens, Greece, standing on the Acropolis, which means "high city." The Parthenon is the building behind us. It's more than 2,400 years old. Isn't it beautiful?

## Για-σου

Yia-sou

(YAH-soo)

# Shalom!

The Dead Sea in Israel got its name because there are no living things in it. This sea has so much salt that everything floats—even Goofy!

שָׁלוֹם

Shalom

(shah-LOHM)

# Jambo!

Here we are at Masai Mara in Kenya, a great place to begin a safari. We can't wait to see the baby elephants!

Jambo
_____
(JAHM-boh)

# Namaste!

This is one of the many ways to say "hello" in India.

Here we are at the Taj Mahal in Agra, India. The monument is made of white marble and it looks so beautiful in the moonlight. An emperor built it in memory of his beloved wife. Isn't that romantic?

Namaste

(na-ma-STAY)

# Nǐ hǎo!

The Great Wall of China is more than 1,500 miles long. The Chinese began building it in the third century B.C. to protect themselves from invasion.

こんにちは

Nǐ hǎo

(nee HOW)

# Bom dia!

The rain forest in Brazil is probably the oldest forest area in the world. It is very green and very wet. The rain forest is also endangered—so we should all take good care of it!

Bom dia

(bohm DEE-ah)

# ¡Hola!

Mexico has many ancient Mayan temples, and we hope to climb as many as possible! This one is called the Temple of the Sun and is at Chichén Itzá in the Yucatán.

Hola
_____

(OH-lah)
_____

Washington, DC

Chichén Itzá, Mexico

Rain Forest, Brazil

N

W

E

S

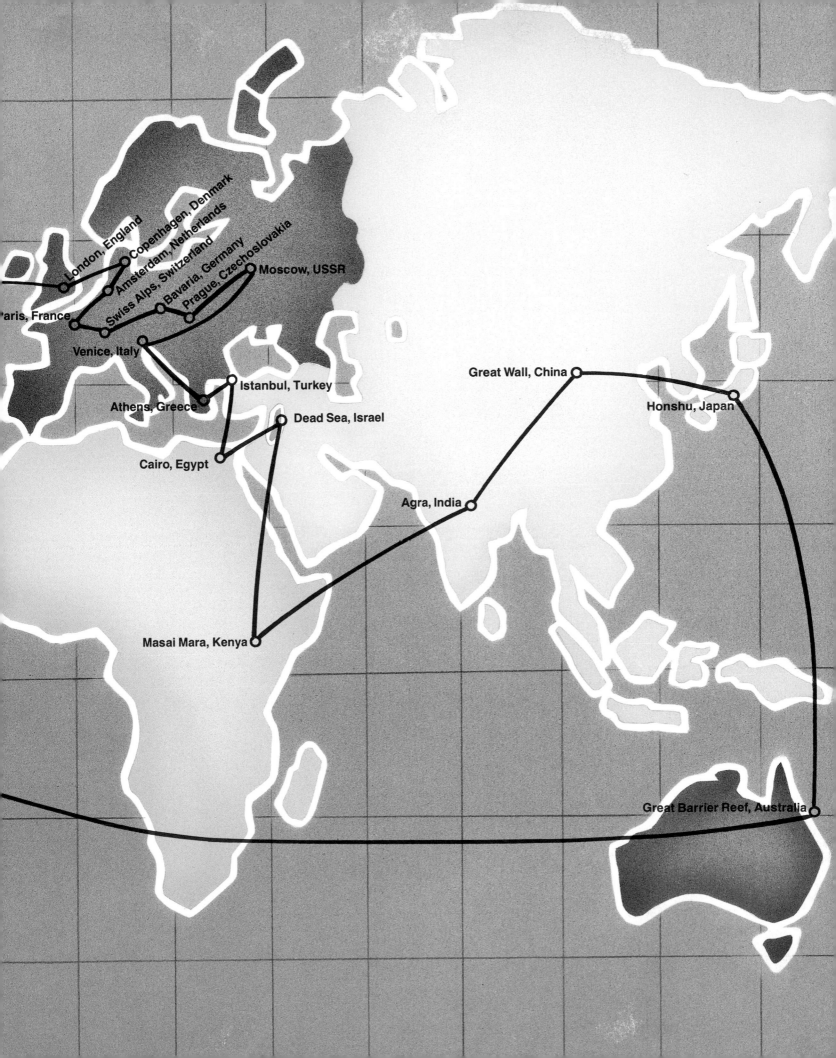

London, England
Copenhagen, Denmark
Amsterdam, Netherlands
Swiss Alps, Switzerland
Bavaria, Germany
Prague, Czechoslovakia
Moscow, USSR
Paris, France
Venice, Italy
Istanbul, Turkey
Athens, Greece
Dead Sea, Israel
Cairo, Egypt
Great Wall, China
Honshu, Japan
Agra, India
Masai Mara, Kenya
Great Barrier Reef, Australia